Made in the USA
Monee, IL
05 July 2022

99104752R00069